Still Becoming

Choose Trust

a Gift for

From

Date

Still Becoming

Choose Trust

50 Devotions

reminders to trust Him daily

#itsaprocess

Still Becoming: Choose Trust

For more information contact Cheri@stillbecoming.net

Published by
Take Heart Books LLC, Toledo, OH
Cover design by Take Heart Books
Artwork by Canva

ISBN: 978-1-958818-05-3 (paperback)

Dedication

Long... Yet So Worth the Read

DEDICATIONS ARE SO HARD TO WRITE.
Getting to this day took so many people. I know it is long, but so worth the read to meet the amazing people who are a part of me. So here we go...

The beginning place of dedication and awe is with God, who is the foundation of the dream. I wouldn't be here without Him. He pulled me out of a pit and changed my whole life. He gave me life and forgiveness. He redeemed the brokenness. He never gives up on me. He is the reason there is a book. It is His, and I'm forever grateful that He entrusted me with the hearts and lives this book will touch. ***This is His book.***

God used the people of Calvary Baptist Church in Williamston, SC and a big, old, purple and white school bus to love me and show Himself to me. There wouldn't be a book without them. ***This is their book.***

My husband and very best friend, Dr. James Garrett. He saw the gifts of God in me long before I did. He has always been my greatest cheerleader and the one who continually has pushed me out of my comfort zone to embrace all God has for me in my process of becoming. There wouldn't be a book without him. ***This is his book.***

My children... Crystal Bunts, Amber Marroquin, and Jamie Garrett. I grew and learned in the great joy and journey of getting to be their mom. Today, each of them continues to inspire me in my journey of becoming as I watch their journey. They are weaved in the heart and fabric of this book. There wouldn't be a book without them. ***This is their book.***

My children-in-love… David Bunts, Ed Marroquin, and Sunny Garrett. Their addition to our family and my life has taught me much as I see their love and pursuit of God, and how they instill that into their families. Their influence in my life is all through this book. This book wouldn't be the same without them. ***This is their book.***

My grandchildren and great joys of my life… Christian Garrett, Aubrianna Marroquin, Carson Garrett, Isaac Bunts, Chloe Garrett, Annaliese Marroquin, Lillianna Marroquin, Eddie Marroquin, Aaron Bunts, Abigail Bunts, Alex Marroquin, Emilianna Marroquin… and my three bonus grandchildren, Skyler Cambarare, Layne Garrett, and Piper Garrett. My life is overwhelmingly blessed because of each of them. I would love to write enough books to dedicate one to each. They make me love growing older because I get to be their Mimi/Gami! They teach me with the lives they live. They keep me young. They inspire me. They are the reason I want to write. They are all over the pages of this book. Maybe not in name, but in heart and inspiration and empowerment. This book wouldn't be the same without them. ***This book belongs to them.***

My Grandmother, Cleo Mackey, who lives with Jesus now. Always my hero, and she lives in and through me. I wouldn't be who I am today without the imprint she made in my life. Her fingerprints are all over me. There wouldn't be a book without her. ***This is her book.***

And then there is this special person I've known from a distance for a very long time that God connected to my life for this moment, in this season. When we sat in a coffee shop a few months ago to talk about the possibility of this book… this project… it was definitely a God connection. She caught the dream God put in my heart and has been such a blessing, inspiration, and encouragement along with being a creative and amazing publisher. There wouldn't be a book without her. ***This is her book.***

So… I dedicate this book to the One who loves me most… my God, my Lord, my Savior… the One who is able to do superabundantly more than I can think, ask, hope, or dream. Thank you, Lord, for loving me and entrusting me with this book.

And I dedicate this book to all mentioned above… and the indelible mark you have made in my life.
Thank you for giving me this book.
All honor and praise goes to God.

Now to Him who is able to carry out His purpose and do superabundantly more than all that we dare ask or think… infinitely beyond our greatest prayers, hopes, or dreams, according to His power that is at work within us, to Him be the glory in the church and in Christ Jesus throughout all generations forever and ever. Amen.

Ephesians 3:20-21 AMP

I am Still Becoming… it is a process,

~Cheri…Mom…Mimi…Gami

50 Devotions for Choosing Trust

INTRODUCTION

Still Becoming... It's a Process

Welcome to the Process!

This has been my life goal: To stay in the process of *becoming*, and to inspire and empower others in their process.

We are ALL in the process!

What is *Becoming*?

It is transformation... a metamorphosis. It is a process... the process of becoming all God designed and created each of us to be, to walk out His purpose and plan for our lives.

My life mission is *to become*. To LOOK A LITTLE MORE LIKE JESUS EVERY DAY. To cooperate with his work of transformation in my life and to take others with me in that journey.

I hope you will join me!

I have many life verses that I lean on day-by-day, but this one is foundational to my becoming journey, and I always like to personalize my life verses and encourage you to do the same.

"I am convinced and confident of this very thing, that He who has begun a good work in me will continue to perfect and complete that good work in me right up until the day of Christ Jesus... the time of His return."

Philippians 1:6 AMP (Personalized by Cheri)

I call this the Completion Process.

As followers of Jesus, we are all in this process, but we can choose to engage and cooperate with the process, or we can become complacent or resistant. That makes a difference in our becoming, and I've found myself in all these responses.

It all starts with being convinced and absolutely sure that Jesus began the good work in us and he will never give up on us.

We must trust the process—we must trust the GOD OF THE PROCESS.

He is going to keep working on you and on me until we see him face to face. His goal is to develop, perfect, and complete us—to see us become the masterpiece He created us to be.

So come along on the journey of becoming with me in ***Still Becoming... Choose Trust.***

I believe there are some special God moments for each of us!

Welcome to the process of ***Still Becoming!***

We are ALL in the process! We are ALL still becoming!

~Cheri

"We are in the process of becoming all that God created and purposed us to be, so that we can do what He created us to do– and that is to effect change in our world and to bring Him glory, all while being conformed to His image."

~Cheri Garrett

1

For Good

God is always working; even when we can't see it. He is working for our best… He is working out his purpose in our lives. He is working and positioning us.

He is always working.

Many times, it might be dark and quiet and uncomfortable, and it seems He is nowhere to be found, but he is there and, he is working.

I love the life story of Joseph.

His family was dysfunctional, and his brothers were so jealous of him that they threw him in a pit and sold him to an Arab caravan passing through, who then sold him to Potiphar to be a servant in Pharaoh's house. Then, through a false accusation from Potiphar's wife, he landed in prison. He helped a fellow prisoner, but then was forgotten… and then remembered. And once he was remembered, he gained great favor with Pharaoh and was appointed as second in Egypt; second only to Pharaoh himself!

Weaved throughout all of this, God was at work refining and preparing Joseph for his purpose and setting it all up. ONLY GOD COULD HAVE ORCHESTRATED ALL OF THIS! He was at work even when it didn't look like it.

He is at work in your life, too… orchestrating all the people and the pieces for you, and for His purpose and plan for your life.

Hold on and trust Him.

It may not look good, and it may not feel good, but could it be that God is weaving it all together *for good?*

You intended to harm me, but God intended it for good to accomplish what is now being done, the saving of many lives.

Genesis 50:20 NIV

How are you choosing to trust God in your life today?

Thank you, God, for weaving it all together for good just for me! Amen.

2
Against the Tide

D*o not fear…* That's what God says.

I would guess that like me, you have gone through some ocean-raging times. We just re-turned from the Outer Banks of North Carolina, where we experienced some storms and the oceans raged. We were on the beach the day after one of the storms, and the waves were huge and violent. They had warnings not to go past the sand bar that the kids always swam out to and rode the waves in back to shore. I walked out about hip deep, and the pull against me, as I tried to come back in, was mighty strong. It took strength and a determination to get back to shore.

The things that come against us in life can be mighty strong, and they want to pull us into fear.

But God tells us, over and over in His Word, **not** to fear.

How do we "not fear"?

How do we NOT fear?

Fear is rooted in lack of trust in God.

To build our trust, we must fill up on the truth of **God's Word:**

- **Truth, that God does not give us fear, but he gives us power, love, and a sound mind.**
- **Truth combats the lies of the enemy that produce fear.**
- **Truth dispels fear and every lie of the enemy.**

Then we allow the peace of God, that we can't even understand, to take up guard over our hearts and our minds.

Fear not!

Choose trust. Choose peace.

It takes strength and determination to push ***against the tide*** of fear and walk in trust and peace.

"For I am the Lord your God who takes hold of your right hand and says to you, Do not fear; I will help you."

Isaiah 41:13 NIV

What fears do you need to submit to God?

Thank you, God, for helping me.
Thank you for helping me to walk in trust and peace.
Amen.

3

Path into Purpose

Do we only trust God when there is no other option? Or do we just trust Him when we can figure things out on our own?

And is that even trust?

Or do we go where He leads us, say what he puts in our spirits to say, and do what he tells us to do, with complete and absolute trust, even not knowing where that obedience will lead? And do we continue to trust when it doesn't look like what we thought it would?

Spirit, lead me where my trust is without borders...

> But I am trusting you, O Lord, saying, "You are my God!"
>
> Psalm 31:14 NLT

Trust His plans! THEY ARE GOOD PLANS.

Following where He leads is an adventure!

It is not a straight path with no struggle, but it is a path of growth and becoming more like Him.

A ***path into*** His ***purpose*** and plan, and a path that causes us to bump into others, where we are salt and light in their lives.

It is a crazy, winding path through mountains and valleys.

Follow Him... it is the adventure of a lifetime!

A lifetime adventure with Jesus!

> Serve only the Lord your God and fear him alone. Obey his commands, listen to his voice, and cling to him.
>
> Deuteronomy 13:4 NLT

Thank you, God, for leading me!
Help me to trust you on this adventure of a lifetime!
Amen.

4

Trust His Timing

God does not live in the time consciousness that we do.

A thousand years, or a day, are all the same to Him.

What He is after—is you and me.

He is not slow to keep His promises, but He is patient to complete the work in us. So, praise Him in the hallway knowing he is patiently completing you. The next door will open when you are ready for what's on the other side.

> But you must not forget this one thing, dear friends: A day is like a thousand years to the Lord, and a thousand years is like a day. The Lord isn't really being slow about his promise, as some people think. No, he is being patient for your sake. He does not want anyone to be destroyed but wants everyone to repent.
>
> 2 Peter 3:8-9 NLT

God's timing is perfect. It is perfect in ways we can't imagine because he sees all. He sees where we've been, where we are and where we are going.

A huge part of trusting God is trusting his timing.

For me, I know that I would have already been finished with this health challenge I face and moved on, BUT, God sees more. His purpose is greater, and he is after more than just my healing and moving on. So, I choose to trust him and to stand in his promises and to ***trust his timing.***

He sees. He knows. He's at work in me.

Trust God's timing… you may never know what He is protecting you from.

"At the right time, I, the Lord, will make it happen."

Isaiah 60:22 NLT

Are you trusting in God's timing?
Where can you lean into His promises and trust that he is at work in you?

Take a few minutes on the next page to jot down your journey of trust.

Thank you, God, for helping me to trust in your perfect timing in all areas of my life.
Amen.

5

Tell Him Everything

Take a deep breath and let it go...

He cares about everything that concerns us, so we can *trust Him* when we cast all of it *on Him*.

He can handle it.

He truly and completely cares for each one of us. The huge thing about casting our cares on Him is to NOT reel them back in.

> Casting all your cares [all your anxieties, all your worries, and all your concerns, once and for all] on Him, for He cares about you [with deepest affection, and watches over you very carefully].
>
> 1 Peter 5:7 AMP

CAST THEM AND LEAVE THEM.

Today, choose not to worry. Choose to cast and leave.

Talk to God and ***tell Him everything.***

Then choose God's peace, and his peace will set up a guard around your heart and mind.

Don't worry about anything; instead, pray about everything. Tell God what you need, and thank him for all he has done. Then you will experience God's peace, which exceeds anything we can understand. His peace will guard your hearts and minds as you live in Christ Jesus.

Philippians 4:6-7 NLT

Are you talking to God and telling Him everything? What do you need to submit to God today?

Thank you, God, for guarding my heart and mind with your peace. Help me to choose trust and to not worry. Help me to learn to cast my worries and leave them. Amen.

6

Songs, Bursting

Some days just don't turn out the way you wanted or prayed for.

I had one of those days yesterday.

Those are the days we remind ourselves that He is always faithful… that He is a shield around us… that He is our rampart. (A rampart is a defensive wall of a castle or walled city.)

He is a defensive wall around us.

So, we crawl up under His feathers and find refuge.

That's where you will find me. He covers me… Selah.

I trust Him with all my heart.

I am *still becoming*… He helps me.

He is my strength. I will *not* give up.

I *will* trust Him.

Because of Him,
my heart is full of joy, and
I ***burst*** out in ***songs***
to Him.

The Lord is my strength and shield.
I trust him with all my heart.
He helps me, and my heart is filled with joy.
I burst out in songs of thanksgiving.
Psalm 28:7 NLT

He covers me! I trust Him with all my heart!

Are you trusting God today to be your shield and strength? How can you trust Him more?

Lord, help me to allow you to be my source of strength.
Help me to find refuge in You.
Amen.

7

His Masterpiece

Wherever you are in your life, however ugly you may feel, or however bad things may seem… there is a beautiful butterfly on the inside of you struggling and pushing to be freed.

You are struggling and pushing to become the beautiful butterfly God created you to be.

Keep pushing!
Keep struggling!

When the caterpillar gets all wrapped up in the cocoon and is being broken down to liquid, it thinks it is all over. But just when the caterpillar thought the world was ending, that its very life was ending, it didn't give up! It continued to push and struggle, and this amazing thing happened… it emerged a beautiful butterfly, flying free!

In like manner, just when you think your world has come to an end, God has other plans.

Plans to complete you; plans for you to *become* all He created you to be.

Push! Struggle!

Keep pushing and struggling until you break free to be the beautiful, amazing, purpose-filled person God has created you to be!

We don't always see the plan... or remember that ***His*** plans are ALWAYS higher.

We aren't always filled with hope.

We don't always see the amazing creation we are.

We don't always see ourselves as a ***masterpiece.***

That is because we are involved in a process… a process very similar to that of the butterfly. A process to transform us—first on the inside, and then on the outside.

Becoming is CHOOSING TO STAY IN THE PROCESS to be transformed into all He created and designed *us* to be.

I choose You, Lord! I choose to become your masterpiece!
Help me, God, to stick to your good and perfect plan...
trusting that your ways, your plans are always higher and better than my plans!
Amen.

For just as the heavens are higher than the earth,
so my ways are higher than your ways
and my thoughts higher than your thoughts.
Isaiah 55:9 NLT

8

Child-Like Trust

Choose trust and stop trying to figure it out on your own.

I can easily move into the mode of figuring things out for myself if I don't see things happening or when things aren't happening the way I think they should. I find myself *not* choosing to trust God.

Surely, I know what is best! And then I'm reminded not to do it my way, but to trust God from the bottom of my heart.

> Trust God from the bottom of your heart; don't try to figure out everything on your own. Listen for God's voice in everything you do, everywhere you go; he's the one who will keep you on track.
>
> Proverbs 3:5-6 MSG

One day, we were in the pool with some of our grand-gifts and Alex, who was about two-years-old, was jumping into the pool, into my arms. He trusted me to catch him EVERY time. He trusted me so much, that when I wasn't even looking, he jumped, still expecting me to catch him. That is a picture of complete trust. I did catch him, thank God for excellent peripheral vision!

God is looking for us to have ***child-like***, complete ***trust*** in Him, just like Alex had complete trust in me. We have to stop trying to figure out everything on our own and choose to trust God with everything we are and have.

Trust Him for the GOD-SIZED plan.

Trust Him enough to jump in the deep water.

He will catch us.

Are you trusting Him for his God-sized plan?

Lord, teach me to trust you and submit my worries. Amen.

Are you trusting Him from the bottom of your heart, or are you trying to figure out everything on your own?

9
Leave Them in His Care

Sometimes it seems impossible to trust… to truly believe His promises.

His promises seem impossible, his plans too big. It seems they will never come to fruition.

God's plans… His thoughts… His ways are always bigger than we are. They are bigger than what we can do on our own.

IT TAKES GOD.

"My thoughts are nothing like your thoughts," says the Lord. "And my ways are far beyond anything you could imagine. For just as the heavens are higher than the earth, so my ways are higher than your ways and my thoughts higher than your thoughts."

Isaiah 55:8-9 NLT

It takes our trust to step into God's plan.

God is calling us to step into His plan, knowing it is bigger than we are, knowing we can't do it on our own, completely trusting him to lead us and work out every detail and equip us to do what he calls us to do.

Today, I choose to trust His plan, to step into his plan.

Today, I choose to cast all my cares and anxieties on Him, because he cares for me and I am choosing to trust him enough to *leave them in His care.*

Choose trust.

Lord, help me to leave everything in your care.
I give it to you, God. I give my cares and anxieties to You.
Amen.

What are you leaving in His care, right now... today?
What is God speaking to you today?

10

The Problem

When we receive Jesus and put our faith in him, he takes up residence on the inside of us.

And when the God of the universe takes up residence on the inside of us, we should have an expectation of something different as the result of that relationship.

He is on the inside of us with all his power and glory and authority.

All things become new. We are a brand-new creation... the old has gone and the new has come. (2 Corinthians 5:17)

Our spirit is brand new! Not recycled!

The problem is that our spirit resides in our body, in our flesh. And our flesh is still our flesh, and it wars with the Spirit of God that resides inside of us.

This is what Paul talks about in Romans 7:19-20 NIV

I want and know to do what is right, but I keep doing what I shouldn't and I don't do the things I should! –Paul

For I do not do the good I want to do, but the evil I do not want to do–this I keep on doing. Now if I do what I do not want to do, it is no longer I who do it, but it is sin living in me that does it.

Romans 7:19-20 NIV

The Holy Spirit takes up residence and starts doing His job; He starts messing with our flesh. He starts the sanctification process, the transformation process; He starts the metamorphosis.

He will never leave us like he found us.

It is the job of the Holy Spirit to conform us into His image.

AND IT WORKS BEST WHEN WE COOPERATE WITH HIM, but it is HIS job.

He makes us holy.

It is His job to conform our soul and mind and emotions. It is a process. And we will not arrive until we are face to face with Him.

We are all *still becoming...*

As for us, we can't help but thank God for you, dear brothers and sisters loved by the Lord. We are always thankful that God chose you to be among the first to experience salvation—a salvation that came through the Spirit who makes you holy and through your belief in the truth.

2 Thessalonians 2:13 NLT

How can you trust Him more with your soul, mind and emotions?

____

____

____

____

____

Lord, help me to cooperate with the completion process.
Help me to trust the Holy Spirit and his work in me.
Amen.

11

Becoming What God Says

Trust is foundational in the process of ***becoming;*** it's the foundation to doing ***what God says*** to do.

TRUST IS A CHOICE.

Choosing to trust God—no matter the situation, or when we can't see the outcome, or even how we will get where He wants us to go, or even when we don't know where He wants us to go—trust that leads to obedience, which leads us to walk out His purpose and plan in our lives.

And during the process
in the journey,
we become—
more and more
like Jesus.

I Choose the Completion Process!

And I am convinced and sure of this very thing, that He Who began a good work in you will continue until the day of Jesus Christ [right up to the time of His return], developing [that good work] and perfecting and bringing it to full completion in you.

Philippians 1:6 AMPCE

In this process, we can set our minds to KNOW that:

- God will never give up on us.
- He is the One who begins the good work in us.
- He will keep working on us... developing the good work He started.
- He will perfect that good work and bring it to full completion.

We are all *still becoming*.

He's still working on *us*.

We are all in the process...

Will you choose the completion process?
How can you start today?

Thank you, Lord, for never giving up on me!
Amen.

12

Three Things

Choosing to trust. It really is a choice. It seems simple, but it is contrary to our fleshly way of doing things… but choosing to trust the Lord with all our hearts… choosing not to run to our own faltered, messed up understanding, but instead, run to God's Word for understanding and wisdom, will make the lives we live full of peace and rest.

As we seek Him and his will, he will illuminate the path for us to take.

I am choosing peace and rest today while seeking and trusting Jesus.

If we can get these *three things* down:

1. Don't worry.
2. Trust God.
3. Submit all our ways to Him.

Then, peace will take up guard over our hearts and our minds, even when the oceans rage and life screams for us to worry.

In the middle of it all, God is right there, and he is working. He will direct our moments and our days.

He will straighten out the crooked paths in our lives.

Rest today in Him. Trust Him. Refuse to allow worry to take up residence in your heart and mind.

Trust in the Lord with all your heart and lean not on your own understanding; in all your ways submit to him, and he will make your paths straight.

Proverbs 3:5-6 NIV

God's got this. God's got you!

Trust Him with ALL your heart!

Lord, teach me to trust you; to lay down my worries and NOT pick them back up.
Help me to surrender my thoughts and my understanding to you. Illuminate Your path.
I trust you to take the crooked paths of my life and make them straight.
Amen.

What do you need to surrender to God today?
How can you trust Him with what you surrender?

13

In the Closeness

When we call on God… when we pray, He is close.

Knowing that takes trust. Trusting that He is listening. Trusting He really hears us. Trusting He is right here with us… He is close.

WE PRAY LOOKING FOR AN ANSWER, but many times we just need to draw close, trusting that He is close, and He cares about what we care about. Trust that He is working even when we don't see the answer. Trust that He knows what is best and, *when* it is best. And just rest in being close to Him.

Trust comes ***in the closeness,*** in the relationship. He desires for us to call out to him in truthfulness.

He already knows.

Tell Him what he already knows.

Openly share your heart… He already sees.

Relationship comes in honesty and vulnerability. Opening up every crook and cranny to Him. He won't pull away. He will pull in close.

The Lord is close to all who call on him, yes, to all who call on him in truth.
Psalm 145:18 NLT

Lord, I want you close. I want to know you more. Today, I want to open up more of myself to You. Come close. Amen.

What is one thing you can open up to Jesus today in full honesty and vulnerability, allowing Him to come close?

14

Rock of Trust

Trusting God. It is foundational to our relationship with Him. A MUST in living our lives in Him and for him.

David went to fight a GIANT who had a sword, and he took his sling and a handful of rocks. He was just a small, insignificant, shepherd boy. And it took only one rock. Why? Because he knew his God, and he trusted in who He is, and what He can do.

And David took a stand.

He trusted in the Lord of Heaven's Armies.

> He picked up five smooth stones from a stream and put them into his shepherd's bag. Then, armed only with his shepherd's staff and sling, he started across the valley to fight the Philistine.
>
> 1 Samuel 17:40 NLT

He trusted Him to conquer the enemy.

He knew the battle belonged to Him, and that He would rescue His people.

What are you battling today?
Who or what, is the giant trying to take you out?

Take up your ***rock of trust*** and let God fight the battle!

Don't take on the battle that belongs to the Lord.

He is for you, and when He is for you, who and what can be against you? You can take a rock to a sword fight when the Lord is fighting for you!

TAKE YOUR STAND IN TRUST.

David replied to the Philistine, "You come to me with sword, spear, and javelin, but I come to you in the name of the Lord of Heaven's Armies—the God of the armies of Israel, whom you have defied. Today the Lord will conquer you..."

1 Samuel 17:45-46 NLT

"And everyone assembled here will know that the Lord rescues his people, but not with sword and spear. This is the Lord's battle, and he will give you to us"!

1 Samuel 17:47 NLT

Thank you, God, for being for me and fighting for me!
Amen!

15

Pressure + Pain + Fire= PURPOSE

What kind of clay are you in the Potter's hand? Stiff and resistant, or soft and *moldable*?

Do we trust him to be the Potter… to mold us, and allow pressure and fire to make us?

It takes trust… trusting that God may use hard things to make us into that masterpiece he created us to be.

I think we all would choose the easier path.

We don't like ***pressure.*** We don't like ***pain.*** We don't like ***fire.***

But they each have ***purpose*** as God shapes us and prepares us and makes us the vessel He purposes; the vessel He can use.

He is the Great Artist Creator.

Just look at the beauty of this world he has created! We are his creation. We are the clay. He is molding, is making us, chiseling us from the inside out. Sometimes we will feel like that clay on the potter's wheel that gets crushed. The crushing has purpose. Our part is to submit to the potter... to trust the potter.

Will you be soft and moldable in His hands, or stiff and resistant? Will you trust Him even when it hurts?

You are His creation; his masterpiece being revealed.

Go down to the potter's shop, and I will speak to you there. So I did as he told me and found the potter working at his wheel. But the jar he was making did not turn out as he had hoped, so he crushed it into a lump of clay and started over.
Then the Lord gave me this message: "O Israel, can I not do to you as this potter has done to his clay? As the clay is in the potter's hand, so are you in my hand."

Jeremiah 18:2-6 NLT

God, I trust you as you mold me and make me. I trust that You are bringing beauty out of the pain.
Amen.

What is God working on in you today?

How can you trust Him more, and cooperate with what he is doing in you?

16
Patiently, Bravely, Courageously Waiting on the Lord!

Waiting can be so hard! The waiting game. We don't like to wait. We want everything right now. Sometimes I feel like I'm always waiting for something or someone...

Waiting can become a stumbling block or a place we get stuck if we don't keep our eyes on Jesus, who is the author of our lives and faith. He is the Finisher.

The work of the Finisher can be compared to the finishing work of a woodworker, when he takes sandpaper and starts sanding the uneven places, bringing out the beauty of the wood.

This is a time of waiting while He is being the finisher in our lives.

We must choose to trust Him in the waiting rooms of life, knowing He is at work in our lives. He is preparing us for what He has for us next... it is part of the completion process, where He is making us more like Him.

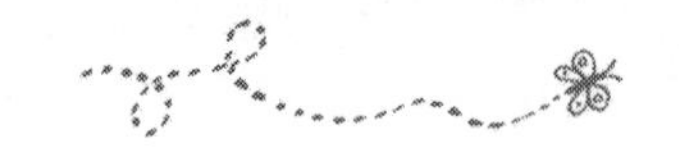

He is finishing us.

When waiting we must:

- Wait ***patiently***. (Man, that is hard!)
- Be ***BRAVE***.
- Be ***Courageous***.

Wait patiently for the Lord.
Be brave and courageous.
Yes, wait patiently for the Lord.
Psalm 27:14 NLT

Don't underestimate what God is doing while you wait!

Thank you, God, for the waiting rooms of life and what you are doing in me during these times.
Empower me to be patient and brave and courageous.
To trust You in the waiting room.
Amen.

Are you in a waiting room of life right now?

How can you trust God in this time being patient... being brave and courageous?

17

Prayer Changes Things

He is the Lord who heals you today. He heals your sickness and disease; He heals your broken heart. He heals your mind; He heals your emotions. He wants you WHOLE.

Believe His promises... stand in the middle of His promises... speak His promises into your life and watch His healing flow in you.

He still heals today, and He wants to heal you!
Prayer changes things!
It really does! Try it!
Need a miracle?
Pray!

He wants you WHOLE!

Our prayers move God.

Prayer produces HUGE miracles and everyday miracles. More than that, prayer produces relationship with God. We share our heart with Him and He shares his heart with us.

The greatest miracle that PRAYER PRODUCES IS CHANGE IN US.

Put time with God in your daily schedule... it will be life changing!

> Then you will call on me and come and pray to me, and I will listen to you.
>
> Jeremiah 29:12 NIV

Where are you putting God on your busy schedule? Write out your commitment to spend time with Him.

____

____

____

____

Thank you, God, because you are the Healer
and when I pray, you will move!
Amen.

18

Even When Storms Rage...

It is well with my soul. When I am in relationship with Jesus, it doesn't matter the storm... it is still well with my soul.

I fall down. I get up...
It is well with my soul.
The *storm* is *raging*...
It is well with my soul.
The doctor report is not good...
It is well with my soul.
My marriage is struggling...
It is well with my soul.
My kids are a mess...
It is well with my soul.

I really messed up. Jesus forgives.
It is well with my soul.

No matter what comes our way, stay close to Jesus and it will always be well with your soul. The enemy can rage war all around you, but he can't touch your soul.

IT. IS. WELL. WITH. MY. SOUL.

God is our refuge and strength,
always ready to help in times of trouble.
So we will not fear when earthquakes come and the mountains crumble into the sea.
Let the oceans roar and foam.
Let the mountains tremble as the waters surge!

Psalm 46:1-3 NLT

May this be our prayer today and every day in all of life's ups and downs...

He knows what is best for us.

I pray, Lord, not my will, but Your will be done.
Amen.

What storms are you facing today? Are you keeping Jesus close?

Read Psalm 46:1-3 again and write down how you relate to those verses. Then remind yourself that it is well with your soul.

____

____

____

____

____

____

At the end, write those words, and then put them where you will see them every day.

It. Is. Well. With. My. Soul.

19

The Storm Will End

Are you in the middle of a storm today? Storms are part of life, and storms have a purpose in our lives, but remember that ***the storm will end.*** And when we call on Jesus, He goes with us through the storm, and He speaks to the storms, and they obey His voice. Don't waste the storm! Let it do a good thing in you... but don't get stuck in the storm!

Call on Jesus and give him your storm.

That day when evening came, he said to his disciples, "Let us go over to the other side." Leaving the crowd behind, they took him along, just as he was, in the boat. There were also other boats with him. A furious squall came up, and the waves broke over the boat, so that it was nearly swamped. Jesus was in the stern, sleeping on a cushion. The disciples woke him and said to him, "Teacher, don't you care if we drown?"

Mark 4:35-38 NIV

Sometimes the storm can be dark and scary. Remember, He is light and in him there is no darkness, so we put our trust in him. He will be the light in our darkness, and his peace replaces the fear.

Choose to trust Him in everything.

Trust Him in the storm.

> He got up, rebuked the wind and said to the waves, "Quiet! Be still!" Then the wind died down and it was completely calm.
>
> Mark 4:39 NIV

> But when I am afraid, I will put my trust in you.
>
> Psalm 56:3 NLT

Are you trusting Him in your storm?

Thank you, God, that you will quiet the storms of my life.
I will always put my trust in you.
Amen.

20

A God Moment

Our natural tendency is to worry. It seems to be our humanness.

These are the times we need to remind ourselves of who our God is… and of His faithfulness and His character. Remind ourselves of all He has done for us already, and put our trust in the never-changing God we know and serve.

It may not happen when we think it should, but it will happen at the right time. It may not look like what we thought it would, but it will be the best way because it will be God's way.

I love looking at time.

There is Chronos time, which is the time we operate in… the time on our watches. We like that time. We can plan for it and countdown to the thing we are waiting on.

Then, there is Kairos time. Kairos time is described as the *right time* or *opportune time.*

For us as Christ followers, it is God's Time… ***a God moment*** in time.

It is when He steps in at just the right time. Kairos time is when God interrupts our routine and touches us so deeply that we are forever changed. IT IS A GOD MOMENT IN THE MIDDLE OF OUR TIME. These times happen often in our lives, and they are the times to look back on to remember and remind ourselves that we can trust His timing… we can trust God.

We can put our worries away today and put our trust in the One who is faithful and loves us like no other.

Forsake your worries! He's got you!

Refuse to worry about tomorrow, but deal with each challenge that comes your way, one day at a time. Tomorrow will take care of itself.

Matthew 6:34 TPT

God, help me today to learn to trust you more. To trust your timing. Help me to remember what you have done and be encouraged that you are working in my situation today. I choose trust.

In Jesus' name.

Amen.

A God moment in the middle of our time!

List 2-3 God Moments in your life that will encourage you when worry comes rushing in:

1. ______________________________

2. ______________________________

3. ______________________________

What are some things you are worrying about today that you need to turn over to God and his timing?

21

Good Things or God's Best?

Overwhelmed? God knows. And He will show you what to let go of and the way to go. But we have a hard time letting go. We carry more than we should. There are ***good things*** we must release so that we have room for ***God's best*** for us today.

When exhaustion and frustration are the norm for your day, it is time… past time… to allow God to show you what needs to go to make room for what He has for you in this season of life.

I'm not sure where you are today, but I would imagine you might find yourself where I find myself some days: overwhelmed and exhausted.

Time for a change.

I want to spend my time in God's best for me.
How about you?

God is the only one who can show us the way to go, what to let go of and what to cling to. We can completely trust Him to lead us… to guide us and to say to us, *This is the way, walk this way.*

> And your ears will hear a word behind you, saying, This is the way; walk in it, when you turn to the right hand and when you turn to the left.
> Isaiah 30:21 AMPCE

What is overwhelming you today?
What can you do to start trusting God as the One who knows what you should do… what you need to let go of, and the way you should go?

Write down what you hear God is speaking to you today.

God, I'm listening for your voice today. Show me what I can let go of today to release the frustration and exhaustion, so that I can walk in what you have for me in this season of life. Thank you, that when I'm overwhelmed, you know the way and you will show me the way.
Choosing to trust You today.
In Jesus' Name.
Amen.

When I am overwhelmed, you alone know the way I should turn.
Psalm 142:3 NLT

WHAT NEEDS TO GO?

22

When Nothing Makes Sense...

Many times, when God calls us and gives us a dream, or a vision, we just take off… and it is not the time to take off.

We must go through the process of being prepared for the calling. We must learn to carefully discern the voice of God and His timing.

When we run off on our own, we are headed for disaster. Many times, it is out of pride. Many times, we just don't understand that there is a waiting and proving season.

Don't follow the voice in your head.
It will lead from your pride and own desires.

We must learn to clearly hear that voice behind us, guiding every step of the way.

This is the way, walk in it.

And your ears will hear a word behind you, saying, This is the way; walk in it, when you turn to the right hand and when you turn to the left.
Isaiah 30:21 AMPCE

I really do love Joseph's life story.

It gives me so much hope and reminders to trust God through all things—good and bad. I often wonder how Joseph's story might have been different if he had kept his mouth shut. If he hadn't blurted out his dreams causing his brothers to hate him enough to get rid of him. Would his preparation not have been so long and severe? I'm guessing his "blurting" was evidence he needed a lot of work to fulfill his destiny.

No matter what, God would still have had to prepare him and get him to the right place at the right time to walk out God's plan and purpose. Also, his story so clearly shows us how God takes our mistakes, as well as the things that happen to us, to work out His amazing plan. Knowing that what the enemy means for evil in our lives—God can redeem.

It is hard to trust God ***when nothing makes sense.*** Nothing.

But that is what is required of us: TRUST.

When everything seems intended to harm us, we press into God and his promises, and we choose trust.

Trust that God is working for our best and His purpose and glory. That he intends it for good.

> You intended to harm me, but God intended it all for good. He brought me to this position so I could save the lives of many people.
>
> Genesis 50:20 NLT

What, in your life, are you struggling to trust God with?
What seems too big?
What seems like it is destroying you, or your family?
How can you choose to trust God in this season?
Trust that He is working all things out? Are you trusting that what the enemy means for evil, God intends for good?

Lord, I don't understand the situations and circumstances that surround me. I don't like them. But today, in the middle of this season, I choose to trust You. I choose to trust that you are working for good. Help me to get still, and carefully listen for your voice as you speak, as you lead me.

In Jesus' name.

Amen.

23

Stop...Be Still...Know...Listen

Be still. Why is that so hard? Most of us are wired to go … to do it all, while God says STOP striving, stop the constant activity, stop going all the time. Just be STILL. Be quiet.

Listen, instead of talking. Put the phone away.

KNOW.

Know that He is God. Really know Him and His character. Know who He really is for yourself.

He is God.

He is Love.

He is Hope.

He is Peace.

He is Joy.

He is all you need for living life!

I'm guessing many of you are like me. You go to bed with a to-do list and many times you can't shut your brain down to rest… to sleep. Then you wake up with that same to-do list that gets additions all throughout the day. The brain comes alive again at full speed for the day ahead… Maybe a cup of coffee first...

What if we wake up and stop for a moment?

Breathe deep. Be still. Be quiet. Listen.

Breathe in His perfect rest to start your day.

The day will come full blast soon enough. We will find it much more manageable when we start it in His presence.

Take a few minutes right now and quiet yourself. Take some deep breaths. Be still. Listen. Know that He is God in your life and in your personal situation.

HONOR HIM WITH YOUR STILLNESS.

Memorize this verse.

"Be still and know that I am God!
I will be honored by every nation.
I will be honored throughout the world."
Psalm 46:10 NLT

Write it on index cards and put it in places you get stressed as a reminder.

Stop.
Be still.
Know.
Listen.
Then... Do.

Where do you need to apply these principles?

____

____

____

____

____

____

Stop... Be Still... Know... Listen... Then Do.

What is God speaking to you today as you quiet yourself and listen?

____

____

____

____

____

24

Undeserved Favor

Today, I want to remind you of some things…

1. **The Lord's faithful love for you never ends… even when you blow it.**

   His love for you is faithful even when you aren't. … When you sin again… when you make poor choices in relationships… when you choose disobedience over obedience…. when you say things that hurt people, many times the people you love… when our hearts are not faithful to Him. He. Remains. Faithful. His love for us doesn't shift or change. His love for us is faithful.

2. **His mercies toward you go on and on and on… They are brand new every single morning.**

   Every day, He gives you a fresh start. A new day.

*Mercy, God's **undeserved favor.** New every day. Never ends. Even when we blow it. He is the God of second chances … third chances … fourth chances … on and on and on.*

3. **His faithfulness is great and perfect and always working in your life.**

He is true. He is loyal. We can trust his great faithfulness to be at work in our lives.

4. **He is your inheritance.**

In Him you have everything you need for life and godliness … and so much more. You only see the edge of all He has for you. The salvation we have in him is all-encompassing. Our inheritance includes forgiveness, restored relationship with him, healing, wholeness, calling, purpose and so much more.

So why wouldn't you put your trust in Him… why wouldn't you hope in Him? Today, I choose to trust in my God who is faithful and loves me like no other… who is always giving me another chance… who is on my side always leading me down this amazing path in the life He has called me to walk out.

The faithful love of the Lord never ends!
His mercies never cease. Great is his faithfulness;
his mercies begin afresh each morning.
I say to myself, "The Lord is my inheritance;
therefore, I will hope in him!"
Lamentations 3:22-24 NLT

My trust and hope are rooted in Him.

What do you need to trust His faithfulness in today? How can you trust Him in that situation?

What area in your life do you need to focus on in your faithfulness to God? How can you start today?

Lord, I am so grateful for your faithfulness in my life. You have been faithful even when I don't deserve it. You have given me so many fresh starts. I want to be found faithful in my relationship with you.
I love you, Jesus.
Amen.

25
We Choose Daily

Are you letting God transform you? God is a gentleman, and he gives us the choice. ***We choose*** to step into God's process of transformation, and every day we choose whether we stay in the process.

Will I go the way of the world… of the popular… of the comfortable … or will I choose the process of letting God transform me?

Transformation changes me. It changes the way I think and it helps me to know and discern God's good, pleasing, and perfect will.

Seems easy.

Don't copy the behaviors and customs of this world.

But our humanness gravitates towards worldly ways. And for Christ followers, it tends to gravitate so slowly that we don't even realize it until we are immersed in the world.

And the world can be like miry clay or sinking sand:
It is harder to get out than to get in.

That is why ***daily*** submission to God's transformation is so vital.

Daily in His Word. Daily in His presence. Allowing him to do the work, to transform us day by day, step by step. To change our thinking process. To change us so that each day we look A LITTLE MORE LIKE JESUS.

When we submit and He transforms our thinking (our mind), we learn to know and understand his will and purpose for our lives. We begin to see and understand that His will is good. It is pleasing. It is perfect. We begin to grasp the awesomeness of God's will and purpose for us.

Choose to trust God and his transformation in your life.

Don't copy the behavior and customs of this world, but let God transform you into a new person by changing the way you think. Then you will learn to know God's will for you, which is good and pleasing and perfect.

Romans 12:2 NLT

Do you find yourself cooperating in God's transformation process in your life? Or do you find yourself comfortable where you are, and unaware that you are gravitating toward the ways of the world?

Are you ready for transformation?

What do you need to change in your life that will allow God to work in you?

____

____

____

____

____

God...I submit to your transformation process today. Empower me to submit each and every day. Amen.

26

What We Truly Need

Are we discerning the difference between a need and a want? That is the real question. I think most of the time we quote this verse, Phil. 4:19, over our *wants*, not our ***needs.***

ARE OUR HEARTS SAYING THAT HE WILL SUPPLY ALL OUR WANTS?

What do we really need? God will meet us in our needs, and He will supply. He will give freely and liberally ***what we truly need.*** He will give out of the abundance of all he has. It may not look or feel like what we want, but He always meets our needs when we take them to him and trust him.

He meets our needs with our best in mind.
He meets our needs with transformation in mind.
He meets our needs *with eternity* in mind.

The big question is: Do we really trust Him?

Do we trust His process of meeting our needs? His way of doing things is far above our ways, far above the way we think. We think from an earthly point of view. We think in the now. **He thinks without those limits.** He meets our needs without limits. His ways of meeting our needs so far exceed our ways. And He fills until full, our each and every need. Just not always the way we see Him doing it.

Do we trust His ways?

And my God will liberally supply (fill to the full) your every need according to His riches in glory in Christ Jesus.

Philippians 4:19 AMPCE

Write the things you are asking God to supply in your life. Then mark which are really needs and which are wants. How can you release *the things that you want* to God, trusting him *with your needs?*

Choose to trust God with your needs.

Trust Him to supply in his way and in his time.

Lord, help me to discern between my wants and what I truly need. Help me to trust you to meet my needs. And help me to trust you to line up my wants with your desires for me.

I choose trust today.

Amen.

27
God Has Got You!

Who is for you? God Himself is for you! Speak that to yourself, and over yourself, and over every circumstance and obstacle you face. Know today that He is absolutely for you. He is on your side. He is rooting for you. He is cheering for you.

So, STOP worrying about people.

They may talk and judge and even lash out at you, but, what can they really do to you that has any eternal affect? ***God has got you.***

Put your trust in Him and him alone.

Anything that is coming against you today, I challenge you to take it to the truth of God's Word. Find His truth about what is coming against you, about what is being said about you. Then, take the truth of God's Word and crush whatever you are facing today. Replace the lies of the enemy with the truth of God's Word and trust his truth.

Trust. His. Truth.

God is for you today!

I challenge you to stand in front of a mirror today and declare the truths God gives over anything that is coming against you! He is for you. He is NOT against you.

And WHO CAN STAND AND SUCCEED AGAINST THE GOD INSIDE OF YOU?

> The Lord is for me, so I will have no fear.
> What can mere people do to me?
> Psalm 118:6 NLT

What are some things that you need to find God's truth about?

List truths from His Word here to speak to yourself and the lies coming against you.

Take a moment on the next page to write down your thoughts and prayers.

Jesus, show me your truth to stand firm on in times I feel defeated or attacked. When the enemy comes against me, give me the courage to speak truth.
I trust Your truth.
Thank you, Jesus, for your truth to me.
Amen.

28

What the Suffering Brings...

After a little while... We struggle with a little while. We want it to happen now. But how much do we truly suffer if it doesn't take a little time?

Suffering is a part of the completion process... the process God uses to make us what we ought to be. Getting there doesn't come by the easy path.

It is amazing to be delivered instantly, but if we are, do we really suffer?

Is there growth? Is there change?

That is what God is after in our lives... *growth, change, completion.*

So...

After we suffer a little while, God does what God does...

The God who imparts ALL blessing and favor, who has called us... He steps into our situation with all His love and mercy and grace and power and...

- He completes us, making us what we ought to be.
- He restores us. Restores our relationship with him which overflows into every part of our lives.
- He establishes us, and grounds us securely. He helps us to grow deep roots in him and in the truth of his Word.
- He confirms us. He confirms who we are in him, and in him we find our value, just because we are his children.
- He strengthens us. Strength that is beyond the strength we see in the world. This strength is His strength instilled in us.
- He settles us. He fixes us secure in him. A steady and secure place. He settles us into this new place in him where we find comfort and security in belonging to him.

That is ***what the suffering brings***.

So, hang in there.
Trust God in the suffering. It has purpose.
Look forward to what comes
...after a little while.

And after you have suffered a little while, the God of all grace [Who imparts all blessing and favor], Who has called you to His [own] eternal glory in Christ Jesus, will Himself complete and make you what you ought to be, establish and ground you securely, and strengthen, and settle you.

1 Peter 5:10 AMPCE

Are you going through a time of suffering right now?
Jot down the things you are struggling with during this time.
How can you trust God in the suffering?
What spoke most to you that will help you in the suffering?

Jesus, help me to receive the times of suffering and brokenness knowing that you are growing me. I want to choose to trust you in the suffering… trust that you are doing so much in me as I submit to your work.

Thank you for letting me be your child.

Thank you for working in me to complete me.

Amen.

29
God Doesn't Make Mistakes

Your worth and value are NOT dependent on what others think of you. Your position in life, your career or job, your financial status, what you look like or how your body is shaped…

God fearfully and wonderfully made you AS YOU!

And His work is wonderful.
You are His masterpiece!

He wants you to fully celebrate who you are in Him.

Your value and worth are that you are His child, and you are uniquely and marvelously created by him... to be in relationship with Him and to do the good works he planned for you to do when he created you!

God doesn't make mistakes.

Maybe you struggle with seeing your beauty and your value.

I challenge you to take this truth and speak it to yourself.

Look in the mirror and talk to yourself. I did, and God transformed me from a shy and unsure person, into a person who sees (at least in part) what God sees in me.

He will do it for you, too.

I praise you because I am fearfully and wonderfully made; your works are wonderful, I know that full well.

Psalm 139:14 NIV

God, I praise you for fearfully and wonderfully making me—Me!
Help me see me like YOU see me.
Help me to celebrate the me YOU created me to be.

For we are God's masterpiece. He has created us anew in Christ Jesus, so we can do the good things he planned for us long ago.

Ephesians 2:10 NLT

You can see yourself and celebrate the fact that God's work in creating you is wonderful, and he wants you to know that fully.

Make a list of the wonderful things God made a part of you when he created you.

God, help me to see me with your eyes and celebrate your wonderful work of creation in creating me.
I am your masterpiece.
Show me the good things you planned for me to do long ago, even before you created me.
Amen.

30

All About Surrender

Letting go can be hard to do. Letting go of people... letting go of things... letting go of having our own way and letting go of controlling things and people. We grasp so tightly, and many times, miss the best God has for us.

We fear letting go of toxic relationships and having no one. As moms, many times we hold tightly to our children and keep them from growing in relationship with God, and walking in the amazing plans He has for them. We hold onto jobs that make us miserable because we don't believe we can do better.

We don't see our value.

God has so much more for us than we see.

Letting go is living with open hearts and open minds remembering that our thoughts and ways are so far below God's thoughts and ways. If we will open our hearts, He will amaze us with all he has for our lives.

Letting go is ***all about surrender***. And trust.

Trusting involves letting go and knowing God will catch you. Knowing He has a plan even when we can't see it. Knowing He is always working for our best, to equip us to do the good works he planned for us long ago.

So, it is time to really trust Him with all that is within us.

Our understanding is limited, but His is limitless. Depend on his understanding. And seek him every day in everything.

EVERY. DAY. EVERY. THING.

We won't be disappointed. We will find our path because He will show us the way to go.

Trust in the Lord with all your heart; do not depend on your own understanding.
Seek his will in all you do, and he will show you which path to take.

Proverbs 3:5-6 NLT

It's time to trust... *really* trust Him.
And let go.

What do you need to let go of today?

List the things you are grasping tightly to that you should let go of:
Is God asking you to let go of any of these things?

Are any of these things keeping you from growing in your relationship with God and following his plan?
What can you start letting go of today? What steps can you take?

Jesus, show me what I need to let go of and show me the steps to take in letting go. Give me wisdom.
Give me the courage to make bold decisions and walk them out, not turning back.
Jesus, I love you.
Amen.

31
Everything Didn't Turn to Gold

What would happen if God asked you to leave everything you know—your family, your security—with no clear direction…?

I've been there.

Years ago, we were asked to walk away from the security of our church… of our salary… of people we loved, and had poured ourselves into, with no idea where we were going to land, or what we would do or how we would financially survive. I struggled and cried and questioned God and he reminded me of what he required from Abram. And He gave me this verse to stand on in trust.

Trusting Him in a different, deeper, and harder way.

> The Lord had said to Abram, "Leave your native country, your relatives, and your father's family, and go to the land that I will show you.
> I will make you into a great nation.
> I will bless you and make you famous, and you will be a blessing to others. I will bless those who bless you and curse those who treat you with contempt. All the families on earth will be blessed through you."
> So Abram departed as the Lord had instructed, and Lot went with him. Abram was seventy-five years old when he left Haran.
>
> Genesis 12:1-4 NLT

He challenged my faith and my trust with these words:

- **Go to a place, I WILL show you.**

  He wasn't going to show us, but was asking for blind trust in him and his plan.

- **I WILL use you in great ways.**

  How? When?

- **I WILL bless you.**

  I'm not feeling the blessings part right now... but He did say I Will Bless You.

- **I WILL make your name known.**

  What does that mean???

- **You WILL be a blessing to others.**

  God, I hope so!

- **I WILL bless those who bless you, and I will handle those who curse you.**
  I really need to trust You in this!

- **Others WILL be blessed through you as you follow me.**
  Sounds great, right? Other than the place, He WILL show us. What is WILL? Where is WILL? What does WILL look like?

Blind trust.

And ***everything didn't turn to gold.*** There were hard days. Difficult times. Struggle. Times of questioning. But we kept trusting.

We kept picking ourselves up and reminding ourselves of His promises, and choosing trust, day after day after day.

And I can tell you that His faithfulness amazes us!
He has opened doors. Used us for his purposes.
Blessed our socks off! WE STAND AMAZED.
And others ***do*** see us as blessed.

It is all Him and our participation in his plan by trusting him blindly.

Is He calling you to step out today in blind trust?
What is He asking you to do?
What do you need to do to step out into the unknown, trusting Him without seeing the full picture?

Lord, give us the courage to step out in blind trust when you ask us to. Trusting You, and your faithfulness.
Jesus, I choose trust.
Amen.

32
Therefore, I Will Not Be Afraid

Fear. It grips each of us at times in life. At times, it seems its grip just won't let go.

God knows the power of fear in our lives and that is why he tells us over and over *not* to fear.

I've never counted the times it is in the Bible, but I've read that it is in there three hundred and sixty-five times! Fear can immobilize us and keep us from being who God calls us to be. It keeps us from doing what He designed us to do. *Fear of failure. Fear that we are not good enough. Fear of what's going on in the world and in our lives. Fear of others and what they may do to us.*

So many fears.

We need to learn to take our fears to God and to the truth of His Word.

Trusting God will stop the power of fear in our lives.

Choosing to trust Him when we are afraid... Trusting Him with all our hearts. Trusting the truth of His Word. Declaring our trust is in God alone, ***therefore, I will not be afraid.*** Fully knowing that no matter what comes our way… what life throws at us…no matter what others say about us or harm they try to bring, that God is on our side and, therefore—we don't have to be afraid.

> But in the day that I'm afraid, I lay all my fears before you and trust in you with all my heart. What harm could a man bring to me? With God on my side, I will not be afraid of what comes. The roaring praises of God fill my heart as I trust his promises.
>
> Psalm 56:3-4 TPT

The roaring praises of God will fill our hearts as we trust him and his promises… and his peace will put a guard around our hearts and minds.

Are you struggling with fear today?

Write out your fear and then write out the promises of God that cancel out your fear.

Take time today to look at yourself in the mirror and declare God's promises over your life.

Give fear the boot TODAY.

Jesus, we come against fear today in your name. Fear has no rights in my life. You give me power. You give me love. You give me a sound mind. I choose to trust you and stand planted in your promises.
Amen.

33

Rooted in His Truth

Perfect peace! That sounds amazing!

How do I get it? How do I keep it?

The foundation to perfect peace is trust: Trusting God with abandon. Trusting His promises. Trusting the truth of His Word.

How do we build that trust relationship?

We spend time with Him. We get to know Him. We dig into the Word and learn His character.

We mine for His promises, and we get them into our hearts and minds. We memorize them and we speak them to ourselves.

Remember… I highly encourage you to get in front of a mirror and talk to yourself.

I do it all the time!

And we discipline ourselves to keep our mind focused on Him and his promises. Fixing our eyes on Jesus. Trusting Him forever because he is our firm foundation.

Is there an area in your life that you just can't seem to stay in peace?

What is it? ______________________________

You will keep in perfect peace all who trust in you, all whose thoughts are fixed on you! Trust in the Lord always, for the Lord God is the eternal Rock.

Isaiah 26:3-4 NLT

Find a promise, or truth, in God's Word that speaks peace to that area in your life and write it down here. Put it where you will see it every day. Memorize it.

____

____

____

____

Now stand in front of that mirror and speak that truth until your mind is fixed on Jesus and your trust is ***rooted in His truth.***

Jesus, help me to push out the distractions and all the things that come to destroy the peace you promise me.
I want to keep my eyes fixed on you and grow deep roots in your truth.
Amen.

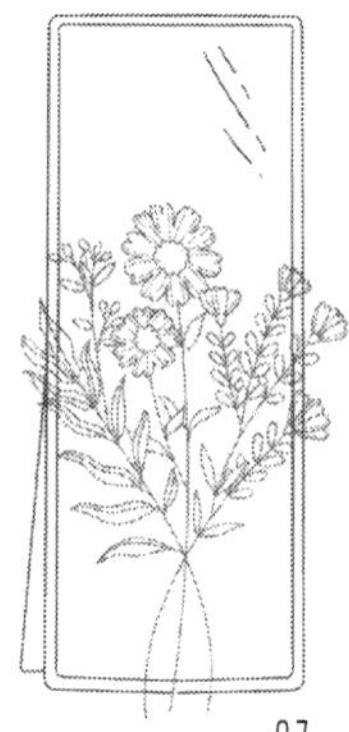

34

Moving Mountains for Us…?

Commit. Trust. And God will act.

Committing our desires… our minds… our needs… our very lives to Him. Committing our will to His will—that is foundational to God moving in our lives.

Moving mountains for us…?

It starts with committing all to Him.

Committing doesn't happen without trust!

Trusting that God knows what is best and that he is working that best in our lives. Trusting enough to let go of the things we hold onto too tightly. Trusting his timing. Trusting that his promises are true and trusting that they are for us.

I've struggled before with trusting that His promises are for me.

I could trust for everyone *but me.*

It can be hard to let go. Trusting is not always easy and is not for the faint of heart.

Yet, committing and trusting moves God to act in our behalf.

I've found myself holding tightly to things I needed to let go… sometimes it is people… sometimes for me it has been letting go of the church, and people I loved, to get to what God had planned for me next.

Sometimes we just have to let go.

Commit. Trust.

And watch what God does!

> Commit your way to the Lord. Trust in Him also and He will do it.
>
> Psalm 37:5 AMP

What do you hold too tightly?
Write a prayer of letting go....

Lord, give us the courage to step out in blind trust when you ask us to.

Trusting you and your faithfulness.

Jesus, I choose trust.

Amen.

35

When I Acknowledge Him...

Alone time is good. I need it many times. But never totally alone. God is with me wherever I go.

He actually goes before, walks beside me, AND he has my back.

He never leaves me alone!

Never abandons me.

He is always right there, even when I don't acknowledge him.

Knowing He is there enables me to be strong, to be courageous… because he is my strength. He is my courage. When I know He is right there, fear has no place! There is no room for fear when God fills my space.

He's got me.

When I acknowledge Him and invite him into my space, into areas of discouragement, he brings encouragement and courage to keep on keeping on.

Today is a great day to invite Him into your "stuff" and take on his strength and be courageous in pushing out fear and discouragement.

He is with you.

Trust His presence in your life.

"This is my command—be strong and courageous! Do not be afraid or discouraged. For the Lord your God is with you wherever you go."

Joshua 1:9 NLT

Where are you dealing with discouragement today? How can you choose to be strong and courageous in your situation today? Remind yourself today that God is with you!
Write a reminder here that God is with you in the middle of your "stuff."

Lord, help me be strong and courageous today. You know I've been facing seemingly overwhelming situations. I choose not to fear, not to be discouraged because you are with me. I'm trusting you. Amen.

36

Ask. Believe. No Doubt.

PRAY. BELIEVE. NO doubt. TRUST GOD.

Believing for that mountain to move, even when it is seemingly immovable…

Most times, we look at the mountain and start trying to figure out on our own how to go around it, or over it.

Do we consider talking to the mountain? Do we believe what God says, that we can speak to the mountain?

God's word says, *if with no doubt, believing in what we say will happen, it will happen.*

We can speak to the mountain, and the mountain has to move.

I have a couple of mountains right now, and honestly, I just keep trying to work *with* them and *around* them. Instead, I need to trust God and what he says. I need to speak to those mountains!

It is the same with our prayers.

Ask. Believe. No doubt.

Watch God move on our behalf! Trust God to do what he says he will do!

Unshakable faith.

NOW THE MOUNTAIN MAY NOT GO the way we want to see it go. The prayer may be answered different than what we thought. The timing will be God's impeccable timing. Speak to the mountain.

Pray. Believe. No doubt. Trust God.

Trusting Him is the best way to live!

> "Truly, I say to you, whoever says to this mountain, 'Be taken up and thrown into the sea,' and does not doubt in his heart, but believes that what he says will come to pass, it will be done for him. Therefore I tell you, whatever you ask in prayer, believe that you have received it, and it will be yours."
>
> Mark 11:23-24 ESV

What mountain are you facing today?

SPEAK to your mountain with TRUTH from God's Word.

Write it out here.
Write out that prayer that you have been afraid to pray.

Holy Spirit, empower me to speak to those mountains with no doubt that they will have to move. I sense you leading me to pray a prayer that will only happen if you open doors and make the connections.
Give me the courage to trust you and wait patiently.
Amen.

37

Glory to Glory

> The journey of becoming is difficult at times, but we must struggle with it, because it is in the struggle that we "become."
> ~Cheri Garrett

Let's look at butterflies!

Aren't they beautiful? Aren't they amazing? I love to watch them and have even planted some flowers to attract them. My spirit relates to them… to the way God created them… the process of transformation… metamorphosis… to *becoming*.

As one who is *still becoming*, I love the beauty in the journey of the caterpillar as it becomes what it is destined to be: a beautiful butterfly flying high. I love that God gives us some amazing pictures in His creation, and the metamorphosis of the butterfly is amazing! It is a perfect picture of the process through which we journey to become all that God created us to be.

> Don't copy the behavior and customs of this world, but let God transform you into a new person by changing the way you think. Then you will learn to know God's will for you, which is good and pleasing and perfect.
> Romans 12:2 NLT

The journey to becoming who God created and designed us to be... I'm on the journey to be transformed. He is changing the way I think.

We are all in the process of becoming who God designed and created us to be so that we can do what He created us to do... and that is to effect change in our world and bring Him glory all the while being conformed to His image.

The process of becoming starts at the very moment we put our faith in Jesus, receiving his sacrifice and his forgiveness, which brings us into relationship with him.

I am convinced and confident of this very thing, that He who has begun a good work in you will (continue to) perfect and complete it until the day of Christ Jesus (the time of His return).
Philippians 1:6 AMP

At that moment, the Holy Spirit takes up residence on the inside of us, and the transformation process begins—the process of making us like Him. When we receive Jesus, our spirit becomes brand new, and that relationship we were created for is activated, and transformation begins.

And we all, with unveiled face, continually seeing as in a mirror the glory of the Lord, are progressively being transformed into His image from (one degree of) glory to (even more) glory, which comes from the Lord, (who is) the Spirit.
2 Corinthians 3:18 AMP

Becoming... it's a process; a LIFELONG PROCESS.

He's still working on me. We are all *still becoming*...

When we receive Jesus and His sacrifice, the veil is taken away and we step into freedom. The veil covered our hearts and kept us in bondage; kept us from understanding the truth. When we turn to the Lord, the veil is taken away. We are free from the bondage of not understanding the truth. Then we can see and reflect the glory of the Lord.

THIS IS THE TRANSFORMATION PROCESS.

Paul is telling us that when we are saved, the veil—*bondage, ignorance, being blinded to the truth, having hardened hearts*—all that was keeping us from beholding Christ's glory is removed and that by beholding Christ's glory—we are transformed. The Lord makes us more and more like him as we are progressively being transformed into His image—from one degree of glory to even more glory. It is progressive. It doesn't happen today.

It is a life-long process.

Glory to Glory:

- from the glory of the Law (of trying to do it ourselves)
- to the glory of the New Covenant (from trying to make ourselves pleasing to God)
- from trying to keep the Law (unsuccessfully)
- to receiving forgiveness and NEW LIFE that has the power to transform us

"He will transform you into His likeness. You do the beholding—He does the transforming."
Alan Redpath

Transformation... it's a process. A life-long process...

How can you cooperate more in the transformation process? Are you trying to do everything yourself?

Thank you, Jesus, for your sacrifice and for this journey of becoming more like you.
Amen.

38
To the Birds and Flowers and to You

We worry about so many things! Things God has already got under his control. Things he has plans for. He gives us promises, he gives us clear examples to show us how he cares for us.

Never be worried about your life… the things you need. He's got you! We just have to trust him!

I love birds and watching them. They don't worry. They use what God provides for them. They are valuable to God. You are valuable to God. If He takes care of the birds, he will take care of you.

Don't worry.

Trust Him.

"This is why I tell you to never be worried about your life, for all that you need will be provided, such as food, water, clothing—everything your body needs. Isn't there more to your life than a meal? Isn't your body more than clothing? "Consider the birds—do you think they worry about their existence? They don't plant or reap or store up food, yet your heavenly Father provides them each with food. Aren't you much more valuable to your Father than they?"

Matthew 6:25-26 TPT

And then the worry for clothes. We worry and fuss over clothes and spend crazy amounts of money to have the best… the name brands. But look at the beauty of the flowers… even the flowers in the fields that some see as weeds. God dresses them and they come and go quickly.

"And why would you worry about your clothing? Look at all the beautiful flowers of the field. They don't work or toil, and yet not even Solomon in all his splendor was robed in beauty like one of these! So if God has clothed the meadow with hay, which is here for such a short time and then dried up and burned, won't he provide for you the clothes you need—you of little faith?"

Matthew 6:28-30 TPT

Can't you trust Him to dress you?

Many times, as I've needed to shop for clothing needs on a very tight budget, I've prayed and asked God to lead me to the right place for what I needed at the price I could afford.

I've been amazed at God's provision.

So... forsake your worries!
Trust God for all you need!
He is trustworthy *to the birds and flowers and to you.*

Are you worrying too much about clothes or provisions? If so, think about trusting in God for making a way in all things.

Lord, give us the courage to step out in blind trust when you ask us to. Trusting you and your faithfulness.
Jesus, I choose trust.
Amen.

39

Trust God's Creative Power

> Give God the right to direct your life, and as you trust him along the way, you'll find he pulled it off perfectly!
>
> Psalm 37:5 TPT

I love the beach. It is my place of relaxation. Quiet time to experience God. I look across the vast ocean. I see no end. And the waves continually come in, sometimes slowly and other times they are huge and crashing. What stops the water? How does it know where to stop?

There is no barrier. The ocean does what God has directed and created it to do.

It stops because that is how God created it. God created it that way. The ocean does what it is created to do. And I can sit on that beach and get in the water because I ***trust God's creative power.***

What about us?

Do we give God the full right to direct our lives? Giving Him the full right is founded on fully trusting him.

Therefore, the real question is, *do we fully trust him to direct our lives?*

To work the best for our lives?

He will stop the raging oceans in our lives AT JUST THE RIGHT MOMENT and in just the right place. Working all of it in the process of completing and perfecting us.

Choose to trust Him.

Do you give God the full right to direct your life?
Where do you struggle to trust him?
Talk to God about your struggle, asking him to help you to trust him more.

Jesus, I trust you, but there are times I pull back on my trust. Teach me how to trust you completely to direct every part of my life. Amen.

40
Patient Beyond Any Patience

When we receive Jesus into our lives, he begins this amazing, good work of transforming us and making us like him. He keeps working on us day after day after day. He never gives up. He is ***patient beyond any patience*** I've ever seen anywhere else. The transformation is the work of the Holy Spirit. Our part in the process is to cooperate with the completion process.

COOPERATION IS DEPENDENT ON TRUSTING HIM.

Do I trust God and his process in my life? Am I convinced and sure he won't give up on me? That He will complete the work he started?

I choose to trust... to trust Him. When I don't see him working. When I don't feel him near. When I don't understand what is going on, or his plan. When it is painful. When life seems dark. When I want to be done. *I keep choosing trust.*

I choose to cooperate with His process in me. To be confident and sure. To cooperate as He perfects and completes me. I trust Him enough to stay in the completion process.

Are you in cooperation with the completion process? Are you convinced that He will not give up on you?

And I am convinced and sure of this very thing, that He Who began a good work in you will continue until the day of Jesus Christ [right up to the time of His return], developing [that good work] and perfecting and bringing it to full completion in you.

Philippians 1:6 AMPCE

God… I submit to your completion process today.
Empower me to submit each and every day.
Amen.

41

And So Much More

He is Lord… the everlasting God. He is not going anywhere.
He is always here.

Always with us…

He is the Creator of all the earth...

The beauty of the mountains and valleys.

The intricate design of flowers.

The uniqueness of all the animals.

The Sun. Moon. Stars.

The seashore.

The vastness of the ocean. The power of the waves.

The seashells.

You.

Me.

I just spent the last week in the Outer Banks, and am always in awe of the beauty of the ocean and the crashing waves. I love to hunt for seashells enjoying the design of each of them.

The magnificence of the sunrise and the sunset.
And our God created all these things ***and so much more.***

He is Lord of it all, and he never grows weary.
Never gets weak. He is strong and mighty.
He is our strength.
His depth of understanding never ends.

And He is there to give us understanding and wisdom in all things.

And this is the God **I get to put my trust in,** that *I choose* to trust in every decision, every struggle, every battle… in the good times and the tough times.

He is faithful.
He is trustworthy.
I choose trust.

Have you never heard?
Have you never understood?
The Lord is the everlasting God, the Creator of all the earth.
He never grows weak or weary.
No one can measure the depths of his understanding.
Isaiah 40:28 NLT

Are you trusting in God?

God, help me to trust you today!
Amen.

42
Learn to Love the Rain

I love rainy spring and summer days. The woods in our back 40 turn a vibrant green. The flowers are renewed with fresh color and brilliance. The grass is fresh, alive, and green. Everything grows and becomes stronger. Rainy days are necessary. All sun, and no rain, leaves the earth parched and dry.

I believe the same thing happens in our lives.

If all our days are sunny and clear with no rain or storms, we become parched and dry. The rain and storms of life bring growth in our lives if we just *lean into* Jesus, and trust that he is working the rain and storms for our best.

He will bring a refreshing and new vibrancy in our lives through the rains as we trust him and cooperate with his work in us!

Heavy rain and storms bring up the "stuff" that has settled in the bottom of rivers and streams. It brings it to the top and pushes it downstream or to the sides. It is cleansing the streams.

The storms of life do the same...

The storms will cause the "stuff" we've allowed to settle in our lives to surface, so that we can take them to Jesus for his transformation power to change us.

I want to ***learn to love the rain*** and storms that life brings, trusting Jesus to continue the process of making me more like him…

Becoming all He created and purposed me to be.

Ask the Lord for rain in the springtime; it is the Lord who sends the thunderstorms. He gives showers of rain to all people and plants of the field to everyone.
Zechariah 10:1 NIV

What have you learned and how have you grown through the rain and storms in your life?

Take a few moments and write down your thoughts and prayers on the next page.

God, help me to learn to
dance in the rain knowing
you are right there with me,
continuing the completion
process in me.
Amen.

43

Sometimes it Takes Being Crushed

I love to listen to this old song by The Hemphills, "He's Still Working On Me..."

Love the words of this old song: *"He's still working on me, to make me what I ought to be. It took Him just a week to make the moon and the stars, the sun and the earth and Jupiter and Mars. How loving and patient he must be. He's still working on me."*

He never stops working on me. He never gives up. He keeps molding me and making me into the person... the masterpiece he has seen all along.

He is transforming me and there are times that the transformation process is painful. But the pain has a purpose, and he is right there with me in the pain.

He loves me too much to let me stay like I am.

He is the Potter. I am the clay.

Sometimes it takes being crushed...and starting over.

The Lord gave another message to Jeremiah. He said, 'Go down to the potter's shop, and I will speak to you there.' So I did as he told me and found the potter working at his wheel. But the jar he was making did not turn out as he had hoped, so he crushed it into a lump of clay again and started over.
Then the Lord gave me this message: 'O Israel, can I not do to you as this potter has done to his clay? As the clay is in the potter's hand, so are you in my hand.'

Jeremiah 18:1-6 NLT

And yet, O Lord, you are our Father. We are the clay, and you are the potter. We all are formed by your hand.

Isaiah 64:8 NLT

Are you submitting to the completion process even in the crushing?

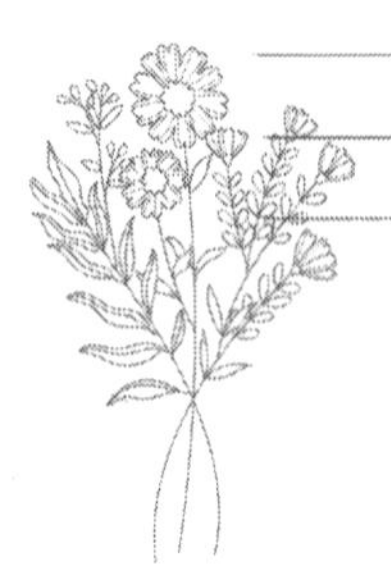

God, I trust you as you mold me and make me. I trust that You are bringing beauty out of the pain. Amen.

44
Get Free From Fear

Are you frozen by fear? Fear of failure. Fear that you will lose someone you love. Fear that you are not enough. Fear of the future.

Fear can keep us from pursuing all God has planned for us… and his plans are good!

But sometimes the things we go through that prepare us, can be hard, and we fear the hard things.
And we fear we might not measure up.

God's Word tells us over and over not to fear.
How do we *get free from fear*?

Prayer is a good place to start.

Take your fear to God… the one who loves you like no other… knows you like no other. He will answer.

He will set you free from all your fears as you *lean into* him and trust him.

Trust over fear.

He will strengthen you to overcome fear and to walk courageously into all he has planned and purposed for you.

It's time.

Trust over fear!

> I prayed to the Lord, and he answered me. He freed me from all my fears.
>
> Psalm 34:4 NLT

What fears will you take to God?

Thank you, God, for loving me like no other! Amen.

45
You Are The Temple

Can you trust what His Word says? This is a powerful truth. He is not just *with* us.

He is *within* us.

> God is within her, she will not fall; God will help her at break of day.
>
> Psalm 46:5 NIV

He is within you.

You are the temple of the Holy Spirit. He is living on the inside of you with all his power and love.

And THAT POWER AND LOVE IS AVAILABLE TO YOU.

You have access to the very power that God used to raise Jesus from the dead.

Can we grasp that? Truly grasping this truth and believing it can change the way we live and the way we minister...?

Believing… *mentally assenting to the truth, and then walking out that truth.*

With Him on the inside, we will not fall.

How are you walking out the Truth of God's Word?

God, I need to trust you and what you are saying right here. It may feel like I'm falling but your word says you are on the inside of me and I will not fall. I trust you to help me in every situation that arises.
You are right here to help me. I trust you!
Amen.

46

The Fingerprints of God

God created each of us with a plan and a purpose. He even works our darkest times into something good. Do we trust His plans? Or do we want to be in control? Do we struggle walking in faith and not seeing the plan? Do we trust in His timing?

Every day we make plans. Many times, our own plans are without God involved.

What we need to realize is that even in making our own plans, it is God who orders and determines our steps.

I'm a planner, and there are many times my plans just don't work out; they don't go the way I planned… the way I wanted them to go.

Then, at the end of the day, I can see ***the fingerprints of God*** all over my day. Keeping me from something. Keeping me safe. Causing me to bump into someone who needed me… *or* someone I needed.

Giving me a *Selah* moment in the middle of the stress.

His plan is always best.

> We can make our plans, but the Lord determines our steps.
>
> Proverbs 16:9 NLT

Can you see the fingerprints of God over your days? How can you pause, in the middle of your day (stress), and look for God to see how he is directing your steps....?

Jesus, order my steps today.
I trust your plan. I trust you!
Amen.

47
Trust! There Is Rest!

So many things in this verse encourages me to trust God.

> I will bless the Lord who guides me; even at night my heart instructs me.
> I know the Lord is always with me. I will not be shaken, for he is right beside me.
> No wonder my heart is glad, and I rejoice. My body rests in safety.
>
> Psalm 16:7-9 NLT

1. He guides me.

I don't know about you, but I need a guide in life, and in this crazy, mixed-up world we find ourselves. He guides me, and I will choose each day to follow his guidance, and his counsel.

2. Even at night my heart instructs me.

Even as my body and mind rest, my spirit is being instructed and counseled and refreshed. I wake up having received from Jesus, even while I slept.

Ever wake up in the night knowing that Jesus wanted your attention? You are pulled to pray for someone. He speaks a word to you. You awake with a spirit of worship. All because he was speaking and counseling and instructing and wooing us, even as we slept.

3. He is *always* with me.

I'm never alone. He is right there beside me up every mountain and down in every valley. Always. In every storm. In every sunny day.

4. I will not be shaken.

Because He is with me, and inside me, no matter what comes I will not be shaken. I'm on the Rock that cannot be moved.

I am glad because He is right here, and I'm trusting him in every step. I take joy in trusting him. In my ***trust, there is rest*** and peace.

Bless the Lord!

How does Psalm 16:7-9 speak to you right now?
Write it out and commit it to your memory arsenal.

Thank you, Lord, for being with me in every storm and every sunny day. You are the Rock that cannot be moved.
I trust You!
Amen.

48

My Immovable Rock

Learning to trust God when you are overwhelmed… I've been in that place for a few months now.

Learning to let go. Learning where to run. Learning to cry out to Jesus when in the middle of an overwhelming storm. I want to let go and trust, but so many times, frustration takes over.

And I try to do it on my own.

I'm learning to cry out to Him when my heart is overwhelmed, and trust him to step into my heart with his peace.

No one else has what I need.

He is my safe place.

My immovable Rock.

My refuge. My fortress where my enemies cannot reach me.

O God, listen to my cry! Hear my prayer!
From the ends of the earth, I cry to you for help
when my heart is overwhelmed.
Lead me to the towering rock of safety, for you are my safe refuge, a fortress where my enemies cannot reach me. Let me live forever in your sanctuary, safe beneath the shelter of your wings!

Psalm 61:1-4 NLT

What in your life is overwhelming right at this moment? Tell God all about it and how you feel. And then remind yourself that He is your immovable rock... your refuge... your fortress... your safe place.

Jesus, show me how to stay in that fortress. I want to live forever in your presence... Safe in the shelter of your wings.
Teach me how to stay in that place with you.
Trusting you even when my heart is overwhelmed.
Selah. Selah.

49
A Place for You and Me

Do we trust Him with our forever? Sometimes we struggle to trust him in the moment… I do, and I'm guessing you do, too. He has made plans for our forever, and he is preparing ***a place for you and for me.***

It has more than enough room.

I have a large family, and although my house is very large it gets very small as all twenty-three of us pack into it. And as the grands get bigger the house gets smaller, or so it seems. We talk about downsizing, but then we think about how much we love the family being in our home.

Jesus is excited about us coming to his home, which will be our forever home. He is getting it ready, and it will never feel too small.

IT IS JUST LIKE OUR JESUS… MORE THAN ENOUGH! And when it is all ready, he is going to come and get us and bring us home to be with him forever.

I think of how excited our grands are when they get to come to our house. Always asking for a boys' weekend or a girls' weekend. I love that *they* love to come and are excited to come!

I believe Jesus loves when *we* get excited about getting to go to his house forever.

Trusting Him for my forever! How about you?

"Don't let your hearts be troubled. Trust in God, and trust also in me. There is more than enough room in my Father's home. If this were not so, would I have told you that I am going to prepare a place for you? When everything is ready, I will come and get you, so that you will always be with me where I am."

John 14:1-3 NLT

Are you trusting God with your forever?

Thank you, God, for preparing a place for me! Amen.

50
We Believe Without Seeing

I will believe it when I see it! A statement I grew up saying in my small, southern hometown. And I still find myself saying it about things today… out of habit.

But how often do I lean that way… waiting to see it before I believe it?

Jesus says some believe because they have seen him. Then he says that we *are blessed* when ***we believe without seeing***.

That kind of believing is planted in pure trust.

I DON'T SEE, BUT I BELIEVE.

What does it mean "to be blessed?"

Good fortune? Lucky? Getting the things we desire?

My scholarly husband translates this Greek word, **MAKARIOS**, as *blessed* with a deeper range of meaning like *enlarged, fortunate* or *favored*—such blessing comes from having a relationship with Jesus, deep enough to believe Him without seeing Him.

It can also mean happy. :)

Believing without seeing brings God's blessings… *you are fortunate… happy… enlarged … lengthy and favored.*

The Amplified Bible, Classic Edition (one of my favorites) says, "Blessed and happy and to be envied are those who have never seen Me and yet have believed and adhered to and trusted and relied on Me." (John 20:29 AMPCE)

Blessed… happy… to be envied... when we believe and adhere to, and trust and rely on Jesus even when we don't see him.

Time to change my saying—

"I will believe Jesus, even when I don't see."

> Then Jesus told him, "You believe because you have seen me.
> Blessed are those who believe without seeing me."
> John 20:29 NLT

Thank you, God, for your blessings on my life!
I am fortunate, happy and favored when
I believe without seeing!
I choose to trust in You today and always!
Amen.

A Prayer from Cheri for You...

I would love the privilege of praying for you as we continue this journey of *Becoming*. Some have just started that journey, and some have been encouraged in the journey. Still, some others are only now considering the journey. We are all somewhere in the process of becoming all that God created and purposed us to be, so I know that we all need prayer.

It gives me great joy to close out this book with this prayer for you:

Our precious Father God, thank You for the greatest sacrifice ever made, the sacrifice of the life of Your only Son, Jesus, so that we could be forgiven and restored to a living relationship with You. Thank you is just not enough.

***I pray** for all those You drew to this book. I know You brought them with the purpose of showing them Your love. To encourage them in the process.*

MANY NEED YOU.

*And for those **I pray** that You will reveal Yourself and Your love to them and they will respond to You. That they will begin a relationship with You and start the journey of becoming.*

***I pray** for those who have been discouraged and beaten up and have wanted to quit... that they will experience refreshing in their relationship with You... that they will be encouraged in their journey to become.*

***I pray** for all of us that we would cooperate with the work You are doing in us... in the transformation, as we become that amazing, strong butterfly... flying free and strong and beautiful... becoming all*

You created and purposed us to be... that we will stay in the process until we see You face-to-face when the completion process finishes the work in our hearts and lives.

***I pray** that each person will be convinced and sure of the work You started in them. And they will trust You as You keep working on them, knowing You won't give up. Trusting You, as You continue developing that good work and perfecting and bringing it to full completion in each of them. (Philippians 1:6)*

Thank You for each person who reads the words of this book and I pray that what You have spoken to them will be a seed that grows to maturity... continuing to encourage them in their process to become.

Thank You, Jesus, for walking with us in this journey of becoming.

I love You and I choose to trust you. Amen.

Still Becoming...
Staying in the Process,

Cheri

About Cheri Garrett

CHERI GARRETT GREW UP IN THE FOOTHILLS OF THE MOUNTAINS in a small, cotton-mill town in South Carolina.

She met Jesus at a young age when a church reached out to the children of the town by picking them up in a large, old, school bus that the church had painted purple and white. Cheri was one of the kids that rode that bus, changing the whole trajectory of her life because of the Jesus she saw in the people of that church, and the way they loved and supported her throughout her childhood and teen years.

Cheri married her high school sweetheart, Jim, and entered the life of "a pastor's wife" at a young age. Their life's journey has had many twists and turns as they followed the calling God has placed on their hearts. They've been married a very long time, and still, Jim is the love of her life and her very best friend. They are often heard saying to each other, *There is no one I'd rather spend time with than you.* Their legacy is their three children, three children-in-love, and 15 grandchildren, which bring Cheri and Jim so much joy and laughter… God's best blessings.

Cheri currently co-pastors Hope Church in Plain City, Ohio, along with her husband. She has a heart for encouraging and equipping women who are in the process of becoming all that God created and purposed them to be. She is a beloved speaker both in her church, and as a special speaker for women, in both the states and abroad. She has been blessed to be the speaker for women's conferences in the countries of Columbia and Trinidad/Tobago. She has also taught tour groups in Israel. Cheri and her husband love traveling and doing mission work as a team, especially by encouraging and equipping pastors, their spouses, and church leadership, as well as helping to build up their marriages and families.

Cheri's favorite times are with her family. She loves to work in the yard in the spring and hosting people in her home anytime. She and Jim love traveling together wherever the road, plane, or boat carries them, and hope these will continue to lead them on many other great adventures.

Thank you for buying this devotional and joining Cheri on the journey of Becoming!

If you enjoyed this book, please consider leaving a review on the listing. This small gesture helps in a BIG way to spread the word of God!

Thank you so much!

Be sure to follow the popular Facebook page

Still Becoming

to engage with Cheri about her devotionals and other upcoming work.

She can be contacted at Cheri@stillbecoming.net for information about guest speaking.

God Bless!

Made in the USA
Middletown, DE
04 October 2023